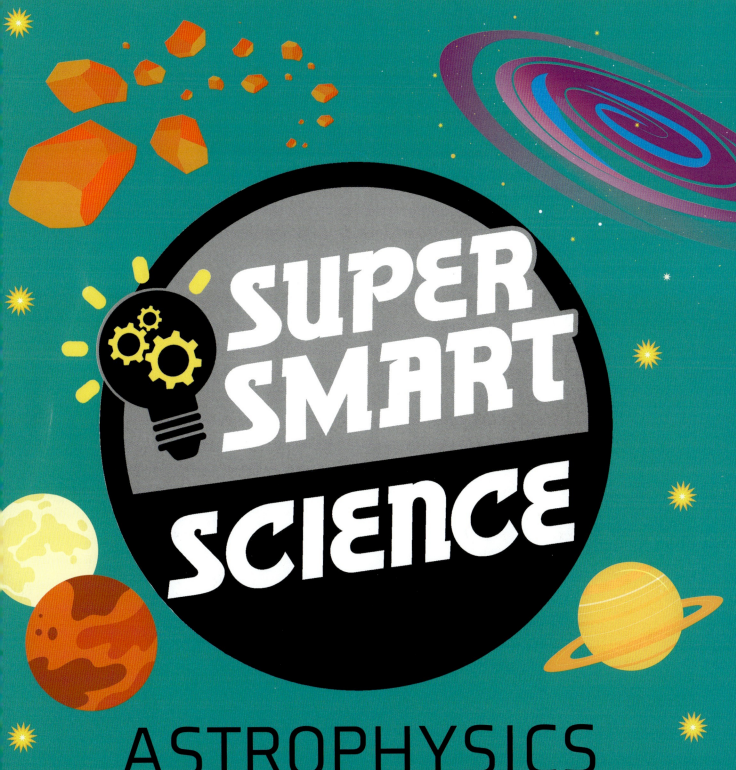

SUPER SMART SCIENCE

ASTROPHYSICS MADE EASY

WRITTEN BY
DR ALISTAIR BUTCHER

WAYLAND
www.waylandbooks.co.uk

First published in Great Britain in 2021
by Wayland

Copyright © Hodder and Stoughton, 2021

Editor: Elise Short
Series scientific coordinator: Dr Alistair Butcher
Science consultant: Dr Asher Kaboth
Design and illustration: Collaborate Ltd

HB ISBN: 978 1 5263 1372 0
PB ISBN: 978 1 5263 1373 7

Printed and bound in Dubai

Wayland, an imprint of
Hachette Children's Group
Part of Hodder and Stoughton
Carmelite House
50 Victoria Embankment
London EC4Y 0DZ
An Hachette UK Company

www.hachette.co.uk
www.hachettechildrens.co.uk

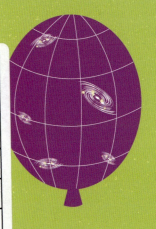

The website addresses (URLs) included in this book were valid at the time of going to press. However, it is possible that contents or addresses may have changed since the publication of this book. No responsibility for any such changes can be accepted by either the author or the Publisher.

Photo Credits:
ESO/L. Calçada,CCA 4.0. International License 27c; ESO/EHT collaboration,CCA 4.0. International License 21t; ESO/M. Kommesser 25b.
NASA & ESA 26b; NASA, ESA, J. Hester, A. Loll (Arizona State University) 19c; NASA/WMAP Science Team 28b.
Shutterstock: Denis Belitsky 24; Alex Mit 25t.

Picture credits: Every attempt has been made to clear copyright. Should there be any inadvertent omission please apply to the publisher for rectification.

CONTENTS

WELCOME TO ASTROPHYSICS

Astrophysics is a type of science that studies things in space. What stars are made of, where planets come from and the fate of the universe itself are some of the questions astrophysicists try to answer. But first, let's get a sense of scale.

THE SCALE OF THINGS

SPACE IS MIND-BOGGLINGLY ENORMOUS. THERE ARE HUGE DISTANCES BETWEEN THINGS IN SPACE, WHICH ARE THEMSELVES ABSOLUTELY MASSIVE.

Our planet, Earth, has a diameter (the distance from one surface through Earth to the other) of 12,742 km. By our standards, this is pretty big. After all, it takes about 23 hours to fly from one side of Earth to the other. This is nothing compared to the scale of the universe.

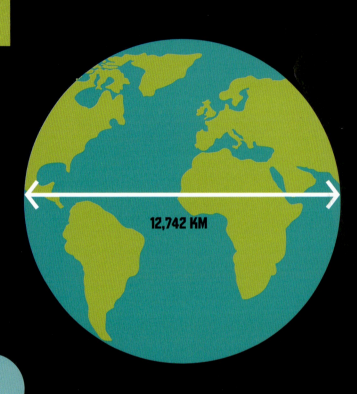

12,742 KM

Earth orbits the Sun, which is a star just like the stars you see in the night sky. The Sun has a diameter of 1,392,700 km, 109 times bigger than Earth's. The Sun is also far away: 148,597,870 km in fact.

IT WOULD TAKE A PASSENGER AEROPLANE ABOUT 19 YEARS TO REACH THE SUN!

EARTH

148,597,870 KM

SUN

The fastest thing in the universe is light. Light travels at 299,792,458 m per second. If you fired a laser at the Sun, it would take 8 minutes for the light from the laser to get there. One measurement that's used often in astrophysics is a light year. This is the distance light travels in one year. It equals 9,460,730,472,580.8 km, a truly staggering distance that's difficult to wrap your head around.

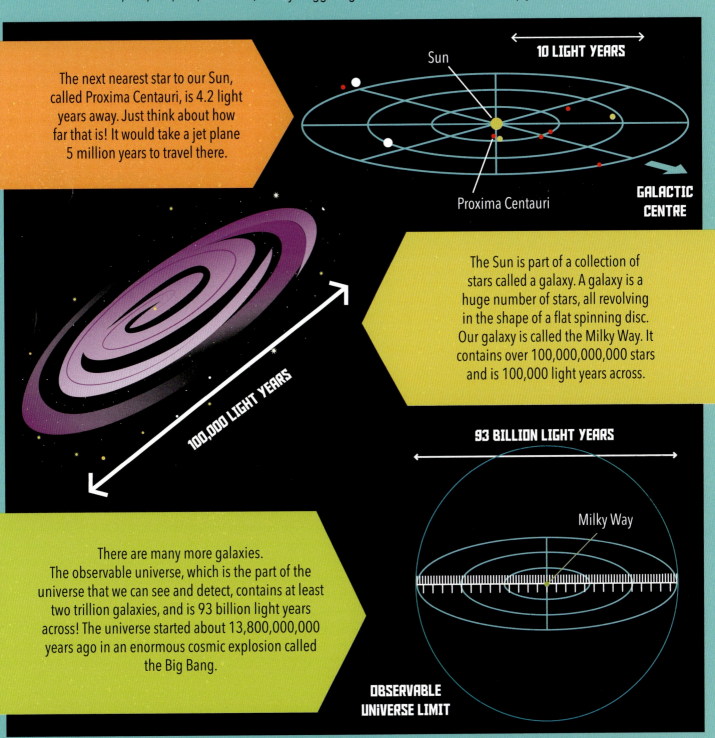

The next nearest star to our Sun, called Proxima Centauri, is 4.2 light years away. Just think about how far that is! It would take a jet plane 5 million years to travel there.

10 LIGHT YEARS

Sun

Proxima Centauri

GALACTIC CENTRE

The Sun is part of a collection of stars called a galaxy. A galaxy is a huge number of stars, all revolving in the shape of a flat spinning disc. Our galaxy is called the Milky Way. It contains over 100,000,000,000 stars and is 100,000 light years across.

100,000 LIGHT YEARS

93 BILLION LIGHT YEARS

Milky Way

There are many more galaxies. The observable universe, which is the part of the universe that we can see and detect, contains at least two trillion galaxies, and is 93 billion light years across! The universe started about 13,800,000,000 years ago in an enormous cosmic explosion called the Big Bang.

OBSERVABLE UNIVERSE LIMIT

Scientists have a way of writing these enormous numbers that saves a lot of ink and space. It's called scientific notation. The age of the universe in scientific notation would be 1.38×10^{10} years.

With such astounding numbers of stars and galaxies, and such enormous distances, there are undoubtedly countless wonders and marvels to observe. So let's get started.

WHAT IS GRAVITY?

Before we can think about stars, we first need to understand a very important phenomenon. When you hold out an object, such as an apple, and let go of it, the apple will fall to the floor. The apple falls because of something called gravity. Gravity is the thing that keeps you grounded on Earth and controls the motion of everything in space. It's the thing that both makes objects fall and the moon orbit Earth. So, what is gravity?

Physicist Albert Einstein (1879–1955) came up with our current theory of gravity between 1907 and 1915. It's called general relativity. He discovered that anything with a **mass** bends and warps both space and time, which he combined and called space-time, around itself. This is a mind-bending concept that scientists have been trying to wrap their head around for over a century.

SO, WHAT IS MASS?

AN OBJECT WITH MASS RESISTS CHANGES TO ITS MOTION. THE MORE MASS SOMETHING HAS, THE MORE DIFFICULT IT IS TO PUSH AROUND.

AND WHAT IS SPACE-TIME?

IT IS SOMETHING CALLED A CO-ORDINATE SYSTEM, WHICH IS A WAY OF MEASURING EXACTLY WHERE SOMETHING IS.

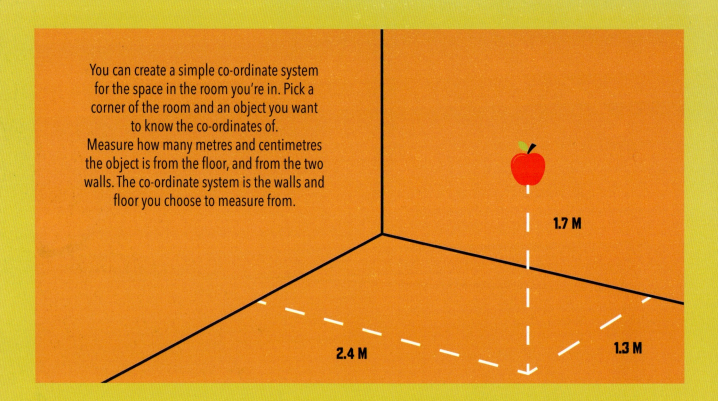

You can create a simple co-ordinate system for the space in the room you're in. Pick a corner of the room and an object you want to know the co-ordinates of. Measure how many metres and centimetres the object is from the floor, and from the two walls. The co-ordinate system is the walls and floor you choose to measure from.

1.7 M

2.4 M

1.3 M

THIS IS CALLED A THREE-DIMENSIONAL CO-ORDINATE SYSTEM, BECAUSE IT TAKES THREE MEASUREMENTS TO FIGURE OUT WHERE SOMETHING IS IN SPACE.

WHAT ABOUT TIME?

All you have to do is add the time when the object was at each position. Now you know where something is and also when it was there. If something isn't moving its space co-ordinates won't change, but its time co-ordinate will keep ticking along. If something is moving, both its space and its time co-ordinates will change. If you let the object fall to the ground and plot the height co-ordinate against the tick of the clock, you'd get something like this:

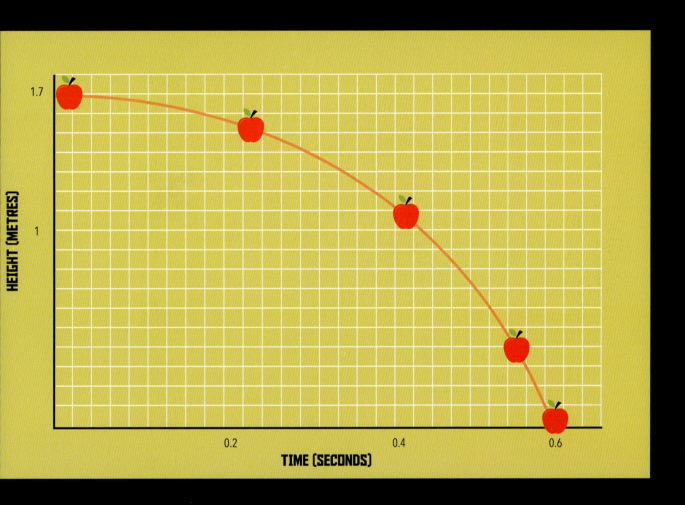

The squares running horizontally represent an equal fraction of a second. If you add the other three co-ordinates, which isn't really possible on paper, you will have the full space-time co-ordinates of the apple.

SO WHAT DOES BENDING SPACE-TIME MEAN?

The three distance measurements of space and the speed of the tick of the clock will change in the presence of mass. The grid in the picture above will change shape. Let's take a closer look.

BENDING SPACE-TIME

According to general relativity, things move along something called a **geodesic**, the line which is the shortest distance between two points. A good illustration would be making a cone. Cut out a semi-circle of paper and draw a straight line across it. This is a geodesic of the semi-circle.

Now shape the piece of paper into a cone. You'll see that the line is no longer straight! However, from the line's point of view nothing has changed, it's still straight and still the shortest distance between each point on the edge.

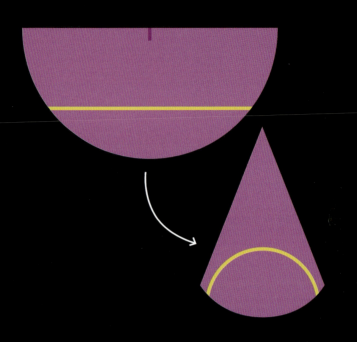

Let's think back to the diagram of the falling object on page 7. It's path doesn't look like a straight line. However, from the viewpoint of the falling object, space-time looks like this:

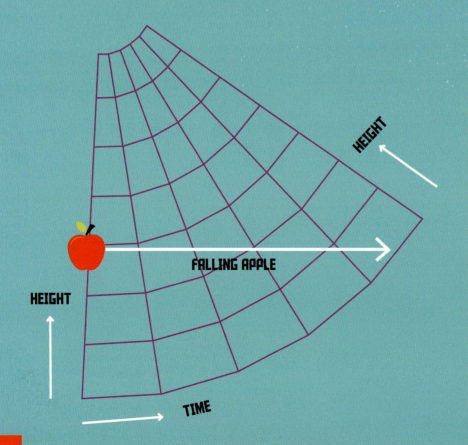

HEIGHT

FALLING APPLE

HEIGHT

TIME

The path of the falling apple is its geodesic, a straight line moving through curved space. The mass of Earth has bent space and time so much that the future of the apple is down! Don't worry if you're having difficulty wrapping your head around this, even physicists have trouble. There's some very advanced mathematics that goes into working this out.

You may also notice that the warped squares in the previous diagram are no longer all the same width. They seem to get wider at the bottom, as if time is slowing down. This is because gravity affects how quickly time passes. That's right, the length of a second changes depending on the strength of gravity!

MORE ON THIS LATER.

Another good illustration of the effect of gravity is a rubber sheet. Here, the rubber sheet represents space-time. If you place a bowling ball on the rubber sheet it bends the sheet around it.

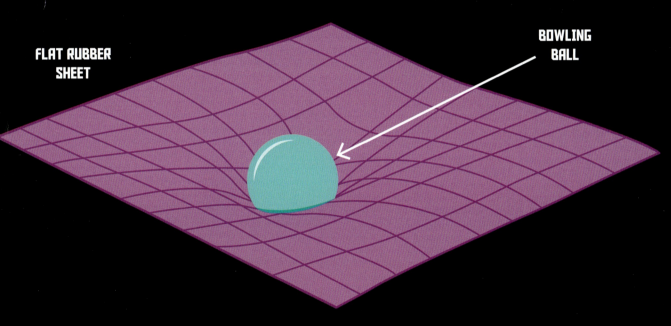

FLAT RUBBER SHEET

BOWLING BALL

So, gravity is the effect mass has on space-time, and the effect is stronger when the mass is bigger. Things fall slower on the Moon because the Moon has a smaller mass than Earth. Think back to the rubber sheet. If you put a golf ball on it instead, the sheet will warp less. The effect is also stronger the closer you are. The rubber sheet is less warped further away from the bowling ball. This means you feel the effect of gravity less the further you are from the mass creating gravity (the bowling ball) – you feel less of a pull, a **gravitational pull**.

Gravity's effect on space-time has all sorts of strange consequences, which we'll be exploring. Gravity affects the motion of everything in space.

IN FACT, IT'S THE REASON OUR PLANET AND OUR SUN EXIST. LET'S SEE HOW THIS WORKS.

STARS

Stars are extremely hot; the Sun, for example, is over 5,500°C at its surface. The middle of the Sun, the core, is even hotter at 15,000,000°C! Our Sun is not special, in fact it's pretty average. How were stars like our Sun formed? What are they made of? What makes them shine?

Everything in the universe – stars, this book, you – is made up of tiny bits or particles called atoms. Atoms are made up of even smaller particles called protons, neutrons and electrons. Protons and neutrons stick together to make up the nucleus at the centre of the atom. The electrons orbit the nucleus like planets around a star.

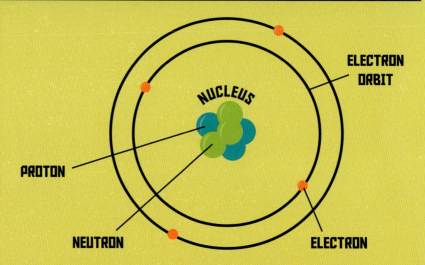

How atoms behave and interact is governed by how many of these smaller particles there are in atoms. The number of protons in an atom defines the type of atom it is, known as an element. Everything around us is made up of elements. Atoms of the oxygen we breathe each have 8 protons, 8 neutrons, and 8 electrons.

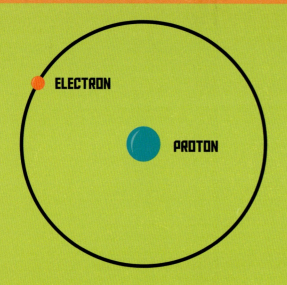

Atoms of the simplest element, hydrogen, have 1 proton, no neutron and 1 electron. Because it's the simplest, it's the most common element in the universe.

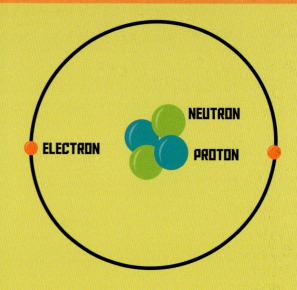

The second most common is helium, which is the second simplest with 2 protons, 2 neutrons and 2 electrons. As a result, stars are mainly composed of hydrogen and helium.

Our Sun was formed 4.6×10^9 years ago. It started off as an enormous cloud of mostly hydrogen and helium. The particles in the cloud moved about randomly and occasionally stuck together to form clumps. Since these clumps had a larger mass than the surrounding particles, they had a stronger gravitational pull. They started pulling more particles towards them, forming larger clumps. Eventually, part of the cloud became a single large ball.

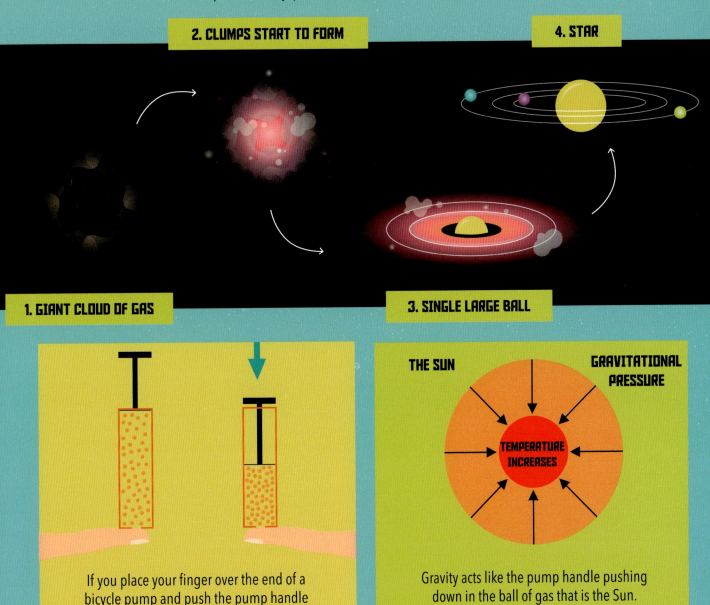

2. CLUMPS START TO FORM

4. STAR

1. GIANT CLOUD OF GAS

3. SINGLE LARGE BALL

THE SUN

GRAVITATIONAL PRESSURE

TEMPERATURE INCREASES

If you place your finger over the end of a bicycle pump and push the pump handle down, the pressure of the gas in the pump increases. The particles of air in the pump get pushed closer together and bounce off each other more frequently. The act of squeezing the pump down transfers **energy** to the air, which increases its temperature.

Gravity acts like the pump handle pushing down in the ball of gas that is the Sun. As gravity starts to pull the particles closer together, their temperature increases. The centre of the star has gas pushing in from all directions – this is where the pressure and temperature are highest.

There are an enormous number of atoms in stars – our Sun has about 10^{57} of them! There are so many and they're moving around so quickly that the temperature in the middle of the ball gets past 4×10^6°C. At this point some of the particles start to stick together. This is a process called **nuclear fusion**. Let's see how this happens.

NUCLEAR FUSION

Nuclear fusion can happen in stars in different ways. We'll talk about one of them: proton–proton fusion. The protons are the nuclei of hydrogen that make up the majority of star stuff (see page 10).

Particles have a property called **charge**. Protons are positively charged, electrons are negatively charged and neutrons have no charge.

What's important is how they interact:

LIKE CHARGES REPEL EACH OTHER.

OPPOSITE CHARGES ATTRACT EACH OTHER.

Electrons and protons attract, electrons repel each other and protons repel each other too.

This means that for fusion between protons to occur they have to be moving very quickly to overcome repulsion, the force that pushes them away from each other.

When hydrogen nuclei fuse, they form a new type of hydrogen called deuterium, with one proton and one neutron. But how did two protons fusing together come out with one proton and one neutron? Let's consider two important laws of physics.

First, **conservation of charge**: whatever total charge there was before an interaction (like particles fusing) must be the same after the interaction. Two positive charges (two protons) becoming one positive and one neutral charge (one proton, one neutron) is not allowed.

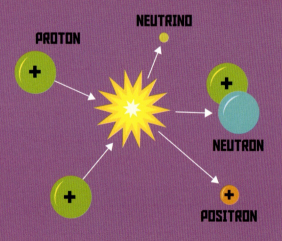

PROTON

NEUTRINO

NEUTRON

POSITRON

This is where the second law, **energy conservation**, comes in. The energy of something is a combination of how much mass it has and how quickly it's moving.

The mass of the deuterium particle is smaller than that of the two original protons combined. Energy conservation means that the total mass at the beginning of the interaction must equal that at the end.

WHERE DID THE EXTRA MASS GO?

One of the protons turned into a neutron and gave off two particles, a **positron** and a **neutrino**. The neutrino is another neutral particle, like the neutron, but with a tiny mass. A positron is the positively charged version of the electron. Combined, their mass makes up the difference.

THIS MEANS THERE ARE NOW TWO POSITIVE CHARGES LEFT AFTER THE INTERACTION, AS WELL AS BEFORE.

Deuterium fuses with another proton forming an **isotope** – a different form of helium called helium-3, which has two protons and one neutron. Just like before, the helium-3 particle has less mass than the combination of deuterium and a proton. The left-over energy comes out as a particle of light, called a **photon**.

The chain continues with helium-3 fusing to become helium-4. A big enough star will have enough gravitational energy to start fusing helium-4. This happens later in a star's life (see pages 16–17).

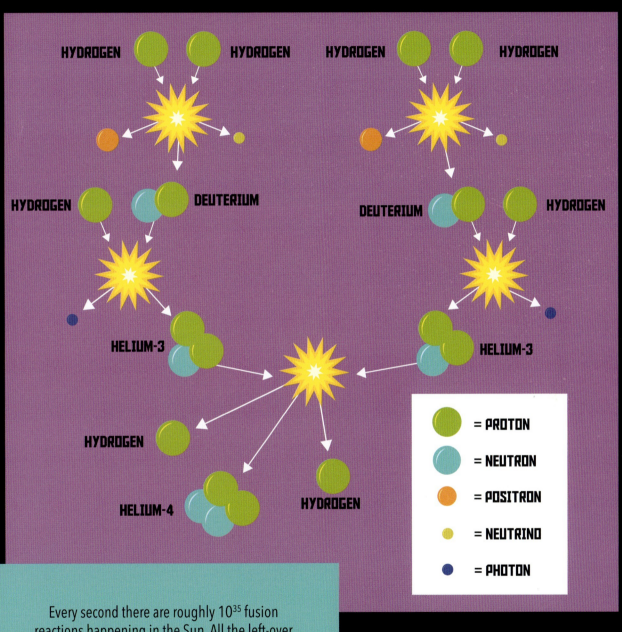

HYDROGEN HYDROGEN HYDROGEN HYDROGEN

HYDROGEN DEUTERIUM DEUTERIUM HYDROGEN

HELIUM-3 HELIUM-3

HYDROGEN

HELIUM-4 HYDROGEN

= PROTON
= NEUTRON
= POSITRON
= NEUTRINO
= PHOTON

Every second there are roughly 10^{35} fusion reactions happening in the Sun. All the left-over energy from these interactions bashes into other particles and heats the star up. Another law of physics states that acceleration of charged particles causes them to give off photons. All those particles bashing into each other cause photons of light to be released, making the star shine.

SO, WHAT TYPE OF STAR IS OUR SUN? WHAT OTHER TYPES OF STAR ARE THERE?

THE MAIN SEQUENCE

The Sun is what's known as a 'main sequence' star. Main sequence stars make up most of the stars you see in the night sky. To be called main sequence, a star has to be part of a collection of stars on something called the Hertzsprung–Russell diagram.

On the diagram, the star's luminosity – how much light it produces – is marked along the vertical axis while its colour is marked along the horizontal axis. Stars that have the right combination of luminosity and colour sit in a band called the main sequence. Our Sun sits roughly in the middle.

The luminosity of a star is related to its mass. The bigger the star, the brighter it is. This is because it has a larger surface area, and therefore more places from which its photons can escape. Of course, the distance has to be taken into account; a star which is further away will appear dimmer. Astronomers have clever ways of measuring how far away stars are so they can adjust their measure of the star's luminosity.

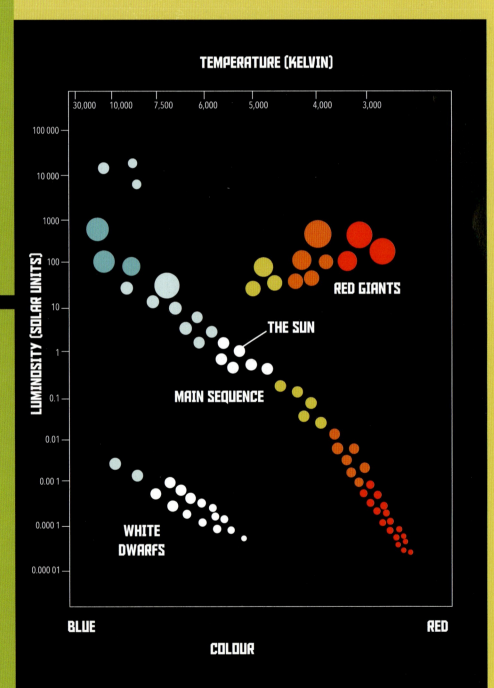

TEMPERATURE (KELVIN)

30,000   10,000   7,500   6,000   5,000   4,000   3,000

LUMINOSITY (SOLAR UNITS)

100 000
10 000
1000
100
10
1
0.1
0.01
0.001
0.000 1
0.000 01

RED GIANTS

THE SUN

MAIN SEQUENCE

WHITE DWARFS

BLUE   RED

COLOUR

WHAT ABOUT COLOUR?

The colour of a star is related to its temperature. The bluer a star looks, the hotter it is. This is because the particles in hotter stars move around quicker than in colder stars. All these particles whizzing around produce photons. Blue photons have more energy than red photons, which means hotter stars look blue.

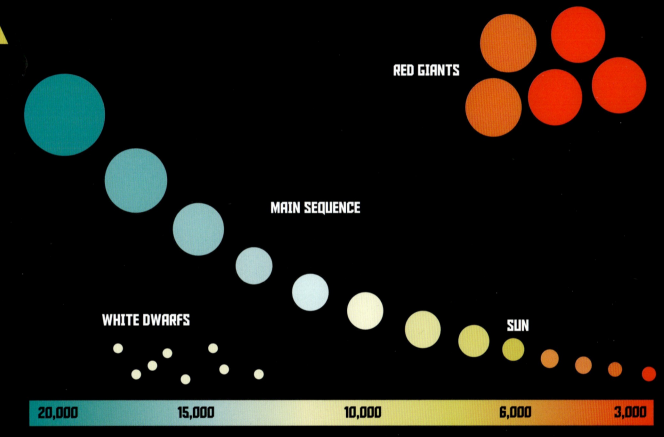

Looking at the diagram for stars on the main sequence, the bigger and brighter they are, the hotter they are. Bigger, hotter stars have more fusion reactions happening every second. This also means that they're using up their hydrogen fuel faster and won't live as long as the smaller, dimmer stars.

WHAT HAPPENS WHEN A STAR REACHES THE END OF ITS LIFE?

You can see this in the two other regions of the Hertzsprung–Russell diagram: the **red giants** and **white dwarfs**. This corresponds to big but cold stars and hot but small stars. These are stars that have run out of hydrogen to fuse and are reaching the end of their lives. Let's explore what they are.

THE DEATH OF STARS

The two non-main sequence types of star on the Hertzsprung–Russell diagram (see page 14) are red giants and white dwarfs. Both of these types of star used to be main sequence stars. What happened to them?

Over time, most of the hydrogen in the core of the star fuses into helium-4 (see page 13) as the star runs out of its primary fuel source. Depending on the mass of the star, different things can happen.

In every star, there is a constant battle between the **pressure** from the nuclear fusion reaction pushing the particles in the star outwards and the star's **gravity** pulling them inwards: this is something called **hydrostatic equilibrium**. When fusion stops, there is nothing to push outwards anymore and the core begins to contract and heat up.

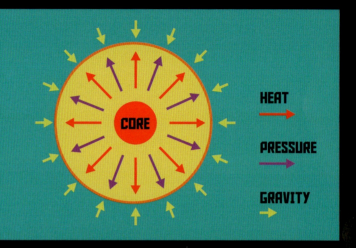

HEAT

PRESSURE

GRAVITY

For stars like our Sun, contraction continues until a phenomenon called the **Pauli exclusion principle** kicks in. This principle states that particles like electrons cannot exist in exactly the same place with the same energy at the same time. This means all the electrons in the star's core are trying not to get pushed on top of one another, and so they have nowhere else to go but back onto the helium nuclei to form atoms. This is called **electron degeneracy pressure**, and it causes a solid core of helium to form.

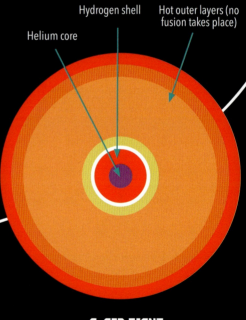

Hydrogen shell

Helium core

Hot outer layers (no fusion takes place)

3. RED GIANT

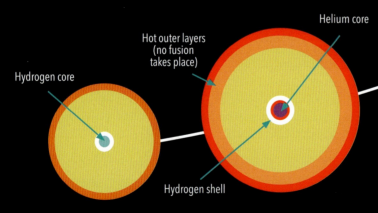

Hydrogen core

Hot outer layers (no fusion takes place)

Helium core

Hydrogen shell

1. HYDROGEN CORE FUSION

2. HYDROGEN SHELL FUSION

The helium core is no longer fusing but is extremely hot. This allows hydrogen fusion to continue in an outer layer around this core.

The increased temperature of the core pushes on the cooler outer layers of the star, making them expand and cool. The much larger surface area results in the star's luminosity increasing. These types of stars are called **red giants**.

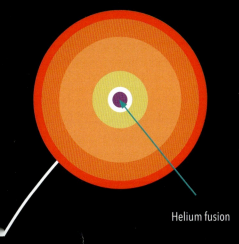

4. HELIUM CORE FUSION

Eventually the red giant's core heats up enough for helium-4 fusion to occur. For larger stars (twice the mass of the Sun) contraction causes helium-4 fusion to occur before electron degeneracy pressure kicks in.

Helium fusion

Once the helium-4 is used up, the core collapses again. Heavier elements then start being fused to form a core. Helium fusion occurs in a shell surrounding the core. The star develops concentric shells, like an onion, of different fusing elements with the heaviest in the centre at the core and hydrogen fusion occurring at the edge. The star is even bigger now and is called a **red supergiant**.

For stars less than eight times the mass of the Sun, this production of heavier elements stops at the elements carbon (6 protons) and oxygen (8 protons). At this point the outer layers of the star are ejected in a big cloud called a planetary nebula, leaving the core exposed. This left-over core is known as a **white dwarf**.

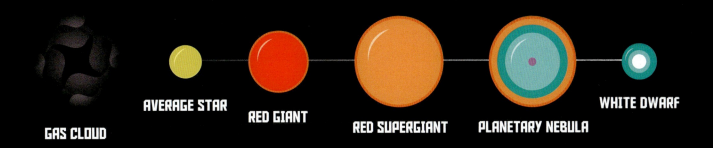

GAS CLOUD   AVERAGE STAR   RED GIANT   RED SUPERGIANT   PLANETARY NEBULA   WHITE DWARF

For stars larger than eight times the mass of the Sun, fusion in the core continues all the way up to iron before releasing these heavier elements in a giant explosion called a supernova (see page 18).

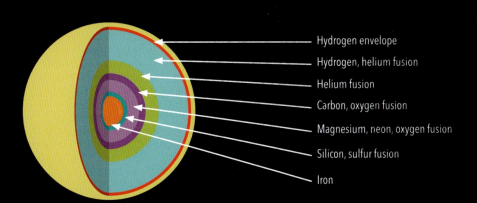

- Hydrogen envelope
- Hydrogen, helium fusion
- Helium fusion
- Carbon, oxygen fusion
- Magnesium, neon, oxygen fusion
- Silicon, sulfur fusion
- Iron

SO, WHAT HAPPENS TO ALL THESE HEAVIER ELEMENTS AFTER THEY HAVE BEEN RELEASED FROM STARS?

SUPERNOVAE

A supernova is what happens when a star more than eight times bigger than the Sun reaches the end of its life. It is a colossal explosion which releases as much energy as 2.5×10^{36} tons of the explosive TNT! Often, they can be as bright as all the stars in the galaxy combined.

This explosion can happen in different ways. We'll focus on one called **core collapse**. Once the core of these enormous stars has fused to iron, the fusion reaction stops. There is no longer outward pressure from fusion counteracting the force of gravity (see page 16). If this iron core is massive enough, the force of gravity is so strong that not even electron degeneracy pressure (see page 16) can prevent it from collapsing further.

The core will collapse in on itself at speeds reaching 70,000 km/s (1.6×10^8 mph). To put this into perspective, a core the size of Earth, which is 12,742 km across, would take less than a second to collapse. During this process, the electrons are being forced inside protons and turned into neutrons. This is called **electron capture**.

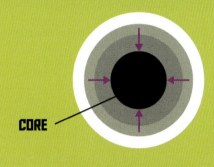

CORE

The core shrinks to somewhere around 20 to 50 km across when it's halted by **neutron degeneracy pressure**. This is exactly like electron degeneracy pressure but for neutrons.

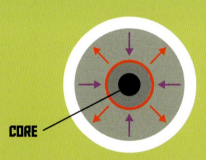

CORE

All of the outer matter of the star, which rushes in towards the collapse, suddenly hits this tiny core. This makes the outer layers of the star start to bounce back off into space.

 = SHOCK FRONT

 = GRAVITATIONAL PULL

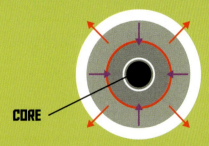

CORE

This outwardly moving layer is called the **shock front,** which starts to slow down due to the pull of gravity.

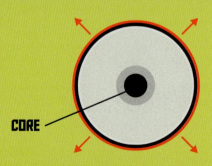

CORE

However, the process restarts and the shock front starts to move again. Scientists aren't yet sure exactly what causes this.

The shock front has enough energy to fuse nuclei into elements heavier than iron. Some of these are ejected into space where eventually they may form other stars and planets. This means that all the elements found on Earth heavier than iron came from supernova explosions.

The outer layers of the star which are blown off leave enormous clouds of gas called nebulae (below).

What's often left over is called a **neutron star**, because it's made entirely of neutrons. Neutron stars are only about 10 km across but have a mass 1.4 times that of the Sun. This means they have a gravitational pull 2×10^{11} times stronger than Earth's!

If the core is large enough then even neutron degeneracy pressure is not strong enough to stop the collapse. There's enough gravitational pull that the core totally collapses in on itself forming something called a **black hole**.

BLACK HOLES

For large enough stars, the gravitational pull of their cores after a supernova is so strong that they totally collapse in on themselves. In fact, there's so much mass pulling on itself, the star collapses all the way down to a tiny point called a **singularity**.

As explained on pages 8–9, two things control the strength of gravity: the mass of the object and the distance between you and the object.

When you're standing on Earth, the mass of Earth is beneath your feet, pulling you down. When you go underground some of that mass is now above your head, so the gravitational pull actually gets weaker. But, with a singularity, all the mass is concentrated in the centre.

So, as you get closer to it, the gravitational pull gets stronger and stronger. At a certain distance, the speed needed to escape the pull of the singularity becomes greater than the speed of light. It's a law of physics that nothing can travel faster than the speed of light. This means that nothing can escape the singularity's gravitational pull, not even light itself. The star now looks totally black – it has become a **black hole**.

The distance at which the escape speed becomes greater than the speed of light is called the **event horizon**. An event in physics is something with a space-time co-ordinate (see pages 6–7), meaning something that happens somewhere, at some time. On Earth, when something goes over the horizon it's not possible to see it anymore. When something goes over the event horizon, its events can no longer be seen and we can no longer interact with it.

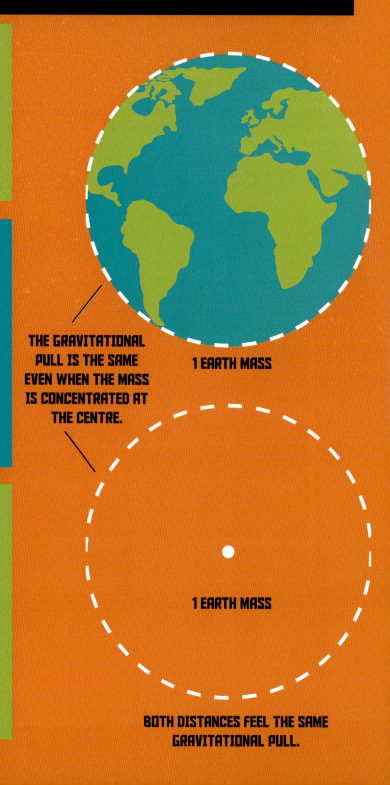

THE GRAVITATIONAL PULL IS THE SAME EVEN WHEN THE MASS IS CONCENTRATED AT THE CENTRE.

1 EARTH MASS

1 EARTH MASS

BOTH DISTANCES FEEL THE SAME GRAVITATIONAL PULL.

We can use the gravitational effect of black holes on surrounding stars to detect them. Stars orbiting a region of space that looks like it has nothing in it is a good indication of a black hole. We can also see the more immediate effect of black holes pulling in dust and space debris around them. As these particles are being pulled into the event horizon, the acceleration is so violent they start to give off light. We call this the **accretion disc** of the black hole.

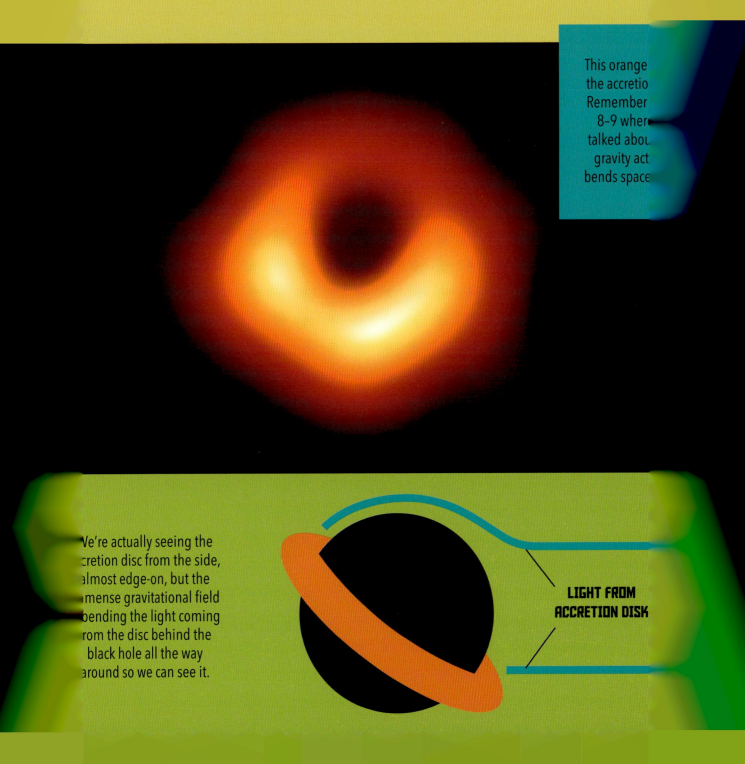

This orange
the accretio
Remember
8–9 wher
talked abou
gravity act
bends space

We're actually seeing the accretion disc from the side, almost edge-on, but the immense gravitational field bending the light coming from the disc behind the black hole all the way around so we can see it.

LIGHT FROM ACCRETION DISK

EXTREME GRAVITY

The extreme warping of space-time around a black hole has some amazing effects. One particularly bizarre one is that time stops when you reach the event horizon.

We saw on pages 8–9 how gravity affects time: time moves more slowly in regions of stronger gravity than those of weaker gravity. This is especially true near black holes. However, it's also measurable on Earth.

The global positioning system (or GPS) used in smartphones and cars that tells you where you are relies on a series of satellites orbiting Earth at roughly 20,200 km above the ground.

Their current time and position are transmitted to your GPS receiver and used to calculate your position. This means they require accurate clocks, which are synchronised with clocks on Earth. However, because they're so far off the ground, these satellites experience less of Earth's gravitational pull. This means the clocks on board tick slightly faster than the ones on Earth. The difference is tiny, about 45 millionths of a second a day. However, this corresponds to an error of more than 10 km to the GPS position! The satellites are regularly synchronised with clocks on Earth to account for this.

Near a black hole, the effect is far stronger. However, the effect is relative. This means if you were falling into a black hole you wouldn't notice time slowing down and stopping as you pass the event horizon. Someone watching from far away though would see you slow down and eventually stop at the event horizon, stuck there forever.

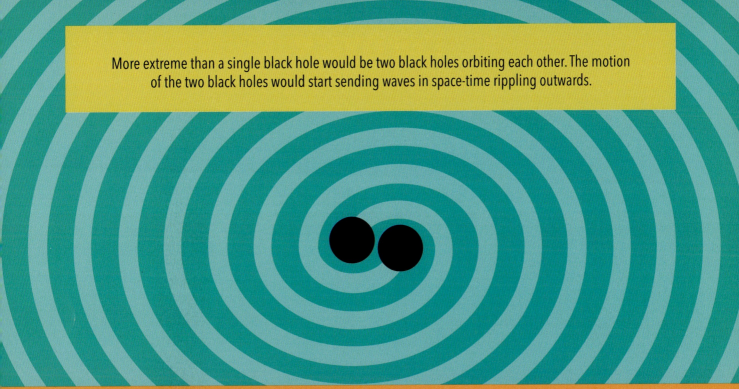

More extreme than a single black hole would be two black holes orbiting each other. The motion of the two black holes would start sending waves in space-time rippling outwards.

These waves, called gravitational waves, are similar to ripples in water when you drop a stone into it. However, they're waves in space-time itself! When one passes through you, you briefly get a tiny bit taller, then wider, before returning to normal again.

This phenomenon was first observed on Earth by the LIGO experiment. On 14 September 2015, the experiment detected a gravitational wave passing through Earth. This was due to two black holes about 1.3×10^9 light years away spinning around each other and finally merging into one.

The nearest black hole to Earth is in a system called A0620-00. It's roughly 3,300 light years away and about 10 times the mass of the Sun. There are black holes much bigger than this, millions of times the mass of the Sun in fact. These are called supermassive black holes and they can be found at the centre of galaxies. Our galaxy has a supermassive black hole in its centre located at Sagittarius A* (pronounced Sagittarius A-star).

Galaxies are enormous spinning discs of stars held together by gravity. Our solar system is part of a galaxy called the Milky Way. If you're far enough away from city or town lights, and you look south at night between June and September, you might be able to see the Milky Way yourself.

The reason it looks like a stripe across the sky is because the Milky Way is a disc that our planet is sitting inside, and you're looking along the edge of that disc.

There are many types of galaxy. The Milky Way, for example, is a barred spiral galaxy. This means it has a straight bar of stars across the middle with spiralling arms coming off it.

The problem is, because we're sitting inside it, we can't see how many arms the Milky Way has, or even exactly how many stars there are in it. However, we can look at other galaxies of a similar size and age to see what our galaxy might look like.

The closest spiral galaxy to us is Andromeda at 2.54×10^6 light years away – next door neighbours in astronomical terms. That means it took the light from Andromeda 2.5 million years to reach us. So, we're seeing what Andromeda looked like 2.5 million years ago. What does this mean when we look out into the night sky? The further away we look, the further into the past we're seeing. If we look hard enough, we can see what galaxies looked like when the universe began.

One type of object we see, typically from 10^{10} years ago, is a **quasar**. A quasar is an extremely bright **active galactic nucleus**. An active galactic nucleus is the supermassive black hole at the centre of a galaxy. It's pulling in so much matter so quickly that we can see the light it emits from Earth.

COSMIC RAY JET

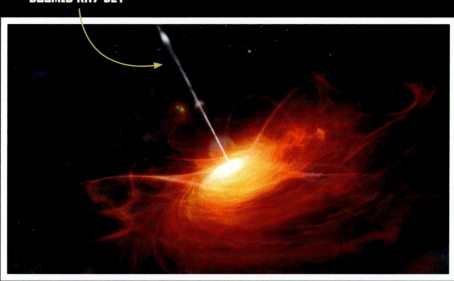

Quasars also give off something called **cosmic rays**. Cosmic rays are high energy particles that fly through the universe from all sorts of different sources. They fly through Earth too, and approximately 10,000 cosmic rays fly through your body every second. There are a lot more in space but Earth's atmosphere protects us from them.

WE HAVE LEARNT A LOT ABOUT THE STUFF IN THE UNIVERSE THAT WE CAN SEE. WHAT ABOUT THE STUFF WE KNOW MUST BE THERE, BUT WE CANNOT SEE?

DARK MATTER

All matter bends space-time. This fact is used by astronomers and astrophysicists to measure the mass of galaxies and clusters of galaxies. The effect is called **gravitational lensing**, where gravity from something massive is acting just like the lens in a magnifying glass, or glasses, bending the light from things behind it.

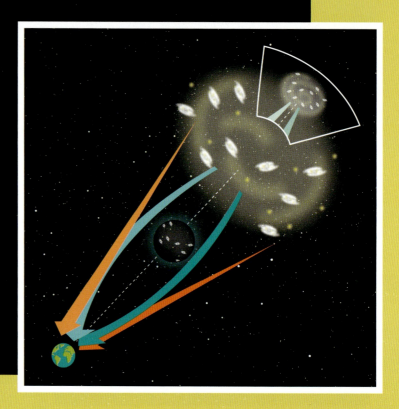

Gravitational lensing creates amazing images when we photograph the night sky.

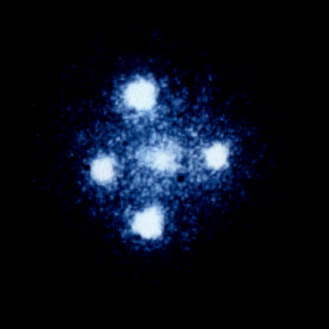

This is called the Einstein cross. Those four points of light are a single quasar (see page 25). The light from it is being bent around into four points by a galaxy sitting in front of it called Huchra's lens.

If you know the distances to the galaxies involved, you can work out the mass of a galaxy by how much it distorts the galaxies behind it. However, when you add up all the mass from the stars in a galaxy, it doesn't match up to the mass measured by gravitational lensing. There's some mass missing! We call this missing mass dark matter.

Gravitational lensing is just one of several ways the presence of dark matter has been identified. Another is by measuring how fast stars rotate at different distances from the centre of a galaxy. These speeds are the result of the gravitational pull of the spinning galaxy, so we can work out the expected rotation speeds given the mass.

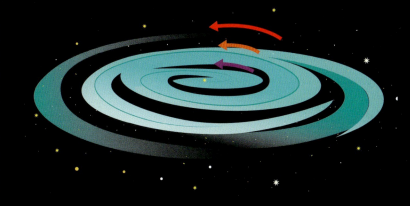

What's measured never matches what's expected and, most of the time, the outer stars are rotating around the centre too quickly. The faster the stars at the edge spin, the more mass there must be pulling them around.

MILKY WAY ———— DARK MATTER HALO

The answer again is dark matter. A huge sphere of it, called a halo, sits inside and around galaxies. This has the effect of adding more mass to the galaxy.

The Milky Way's dark matter halo is estimated to be about 10 times more massive than the matter from stars!

We don't yet know what dark matter is made of. Lots of scientists are trying to find out. It could be a new kind of particle. This particle would have to have mass since it has a gravitational pull. It would also need to be difficult to detect, otherwise we would have already detected it!

The particle would also have to have no charge. This is because it would then start interacting with normal charged matter, crashing into things and giving off light. Again, making it too easy to detect.

Neutrinos are one such particle. They're chargeless, they have a mass and they're difficult to detect. However, they're too light and move around too quickly to form a stable dark matter halo.

For now, all we know is it's there. In fact, there's more dark matter than ordinary matter in the universe. If we add up all the normal matter: stars, planets, this book, absolutely everything, we find that it only makes up about 5 per cent of the total energy (from mass–energy equivalence) of the universe. Dark matter, on the other hand, makes up about 25 per cent! What about the leftover 70 per cent?

DARK ENERGY AND THE EXPLODING UNIVERSE

The universe began 1.38×10^{10} years ago with the Big Bang. But how do we know this? Well, the universe is expanding. When you look at other galaxies in the sky, they're moving away from us.

If you take a deflated balloon and draw some galaxies on it, when you blow it up you'll see that all the galaxies have moved away from each other.

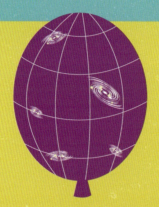
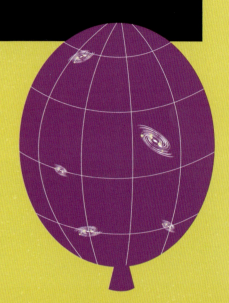

The same thing is happening to the universe – everything is moving away from everything else. That means that if you rewind time, everything starts getting closer together. Eventually everything will be on top of each other.

This is what it was like at the beginning of the universe: everything was stuck close together in a tiny, extremely hot ball. This ball then exploded outwards and everything inside it began to expand and cool down. This allowed the formation of the stars, planets and galaxies we have today.

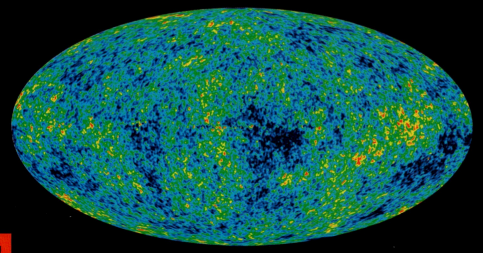

We can still see light from the universe just after the Big Bang. It's called the **cosmic microwave background**. It is caused by photons created at the Big Bang still bouncing around space.

The observable universe (see page 5) is as far as it's possible for us to see. If the universe is 1.38×10^{10} years old, the furthest distance we should be able to see from Earth is 1.38×10^{10} light years away. However, the observable universe is much bigger: 9.3×10^{10} light years across.

HOW IS IT SO MUCH BIGGER?

The expansion of the universe is actually accelerating. Galaxies are moving away from each other at greater and greater speeds. But the **mutual gravitational attraction** of all the things in the universe should be slowing the expansion down. So, what's powering the acceleration? Something called **dark energy**, an unknown form of energy, the effect of which is not currently measurable in laboratories on Earth. With the blown-up balloon, the rubber itself is stretching to make the galaxies move away from each other. The same happens for the universe. Space itself is expanding and dark energy is accelerating it.

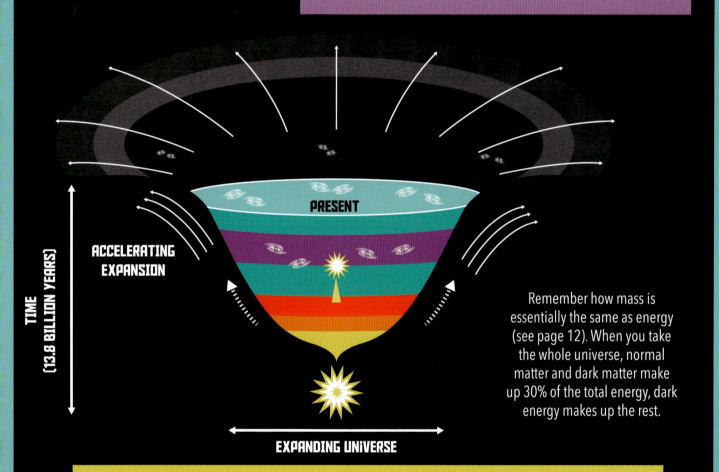

TIME (13.8 BILLION YEARS)

ACCELERATING EXPANSION

PRESENT

EXPANDING UNIVERSE

Remember how mass is essentially the same as energy (see page 12). When you take the whole universe, normal matter and dark matter make up 30% of the total energy, dark energy makes up the rest.

We've only managed to scratch the surface of astrophysics in this book. Astrophysicists have to understand a wide variety of disciplines, such as quantum physics, general relativity, nuclear physics and astronomy to name a few. They build on the lessons learned by physicists across the world to try to understand the universe we live in.

The universe is a vast and amazing place that we're just beginning to understand. Astonishing discoveries are on the horizon, discoveries that you might be able to help with so you can shape our understanding of it.

GLOSSARY

Element
A pure, basic material made up of only one type of atom.

Energy
The energy of an object is its capacity to cause motion.

Fission
A nuclear reaction in which the nucleus of an atom splits into two or more smaller nuclei. This usually results in a release of energy, which can be used to generate electrical power.

Fusion
A nuclear reaction in which two or more nuclei fuse together to form one or more different nuclei. Sometimes energy can be released from this reaction. Scientists are trying to find a way to use it for electrical power.

Isotope
Isotopes of an element are atoms which have different numbers of neutrons, but the same number of protons.

Mass
The amount of material an object contains.

Mass–Energy Equivalence
This states that anything with mass contains an equivalent amount of energy. This also works the other way around, where something with increased energy has a greater mass.

Matter
The stuff that objects are made of.

Neutron
An extremely small piece of matter or particle with no electric charge (neutral) and a mass slightly less than that of the proton. It is one of the particles that make up the nucleus along with the proton.

Nucleus (pl. Nuclei)
The tiny, dense, positively charged core of an atom, around which the electrons circulate. It is composed of smaller particles, protons and neutrons.

Orbit
The path of one object in space around another.

Pauli Exclusion Principle
A physical law which states that no two of a certain type of particle, called a fermion, can exist in the same place, at the same time, with the same energy. Particles like electrons, protons and neutrons are fermions.

Photon
A tiny packet of light energy.

Positron
The antimatter version of an electron. Antimatter has the same mass, but opposite charge, of its ordinary matter counterpart.

Proton
An extremely small piece of matter or particle with a positive electric charge and a mass about 2,000 times bigger than the electron. It is one of the particles that make up an atom's nucleus, along with the neutron.

Radioactivity
An isotope of an element is said to be radioactive if it can spontaneously lose energy by emission of a particle. This could be a high energy photon (gamma radiation), an electron (beta radiation), or two protons and two neutrons (alpha radiation), among others.

Surface Area
The total area that the surface of an object occupies.

Temperature
The average amount of energy of all the particles in something. For example, when you heat something up, you're giving all the particles in it more energy.

FURTHER INFORMATION

BOOKS

The Future of the Universe by Raman Prinja
(Wayland Publishing, 2022)

The Physics Book: Big Ideas Simply Explained
(DK, 2020)

WEBSITES

Find the latest images, videos and news from the USA's space agency, and take part in activities.

https://www.nasa.gov/nasa-at-home-for-kids-and-families

Learn more about isotopes and how they relate to each other in this interactive simulation. Choose 'Isotopes' then select the element to investigate in the top right. Then, drag neutrons from the bucket on the left into the nucleus of the atom on the scale and see if a stable isotope is made.

https://phet.colorado.edu/sims/html/isotopes-and-atomic-mass/latest/isotopes-and-atomic-mass_en.html

$10^0 = 1 =$ One

$10^1 = 10 =$ Ten

$10^2 = 100 =$ One hundred

$10^3 = 1000 =$ One thousand

$10^6 = 1,000,000 =$ One million

$10^9 = 1,000,000,000 =$ One billion

$10^{12} = 1,000,000,000,000 =$ One trillion

$10^{15} = 1,000,000,000,000,000 =$ One quadrillion

$10^{18} = 1,000,000,000,000,000,000 =$ One quintillion

$10^{21} = 1,000,000,000,000,000,000,000 =$ One sextillion

$10^{24} = 1,000,000,000,000,000,000,000,000 =$ One septillion

$10^{27} = 1,000,000,000,000,000,000,000,000,000 =$ One octillion

$10^{30} = 1,000,000,000,000,000,000,000,000,000,000 =$ One nonillion

$10^{33} = 1,000,000,000,000,000,000,000,000,000,000,000 =$ One decillion

BIG NUMBERS!

Here are some of the big numbers you will have seen in this book.

INDEX